Annabel Sutton, BA (Hons), Professional Certified Coach

Since 2000, Annabel has worked as a Personal Life Coach, inspiring people to make positive changes – and to find increased happiness and success in their personal and professional lives.

Annabel grew up in England but has lived in Los Angeles, Borneo and Java and is the author of "The Islands in Between" a travel book she researched and wrote while living in Indonesia. She now lives with her partner Don in Wiltshire and is passionate about organic gardening, wildlife, good food and laughter – not necessarily in that order!

If you would like to receive Annabel's Coaching Tips on a regular basis, please email annabel@life-designs.co.uk

You can also visit Annabel's website at www.life-designs.co.uk

52 Ways to Handle It

A Happy New Year

Annabel Sutton

Neal's Yard Press
16 Stambourne Way
West Wickham
Kent BR4 9NF
e-mail: 52w@winterpress.net

First published by Winter Press in 2003

Revised for Neal's Yard Press 2007

Text © Annabel Sutton
Design © Winter Press

ISBN 978 1905830 527

Printed by Biddles

Contents

Dedication

This book is dedicated with love to Eve Sutton – my Mum and my best friend.

Acknowledgments

So many people have been instrumental in helping me to make this book a reality.

First and foremost I want to thank Don Hartridge – not only my partner in life, but also my tireless Tips Editor-in-Chief. Not only does he do a great job editing the text, but he has a built-in 'Naffometer' which bursts into life when I go over the top or start peppering the text with coaching jargon.

Thanks also to my coach Margaret Krigbaum for giving me the nudge I needed to write this book in the first place. She did that very 'coachly' thing of delicately 'planting the seed of an idea' in my mind that perhaps writing would be a good thing. As seeds do, it slowly germinated until it eventually blossomed into the book you are reading.

Where would I be without my marvellous family – my parents, brother and sister – who, from the moment I was born, have loved and supported and encouraged me to be who I am and be my best. I owe so much to my father who had the innate talent to write, but due to life circumstances found himself on a very different career path. How pleased he would have been to know that his love of and talent for writing are living on in me.

And finally to my many colleagues in the coaching community – who are a consistently loving, supportive and inspiring influence. And to my wonderful clients who are a joy to work with and who teach me new things about life every day

About this Book

In 2001 I started writing regular Coaching Tips, initially for my coaching clients, and subsequently for anyone who expressed an interest in personal development. 52 Ways to Handle It is a compilation of these tips – one for each week of the year from January to December – that you can read in one sitting, each week, or dip into at will.

Whichever method you choose, the main thing is to enjoy the stimulus to thought and action that each tip provides.

Each tip has space on the opposite page for you to write your thoughts or plans of action. Or you may prefer to buy a journal or notebook to use week by week alongside this book.

You could even put together a weekly support group of like-minded people – to discuss and work on each tip together.

I've loved writing the tips, and greatly enjoy the feedback from readers when something has struck a chord and clearly made a difference to their lives. I hope that you, too, will find them inspirational and I wish you great success and happiness in all that you undertake.

Annabel Sutton

New Year – New You!

At Neal's Yard Remedies we've been helping transform people's lives for over 25 years, by inspiring them to live by the principles of natural health. We believe in a holistic approach to health and beauty that means we only use the purest natural ingredients in all our products.

This New Year, we want to encourage more people to live happier, healthier lives – to treat their bodies with love, to enjoy a good diet and exercise and to avoid harmful chemicals in their food and on their skin by choosing organic. By nurturing ourselves with a daily skin care routine and pampering ourselves with therapies and massages we can enjoy the coming year feeling more energetic and rejuvenated.

Annabel Sutton is a renowned Personal Life Coach who has helped many people to put aside their doubts and pursue their dreams. We hope you'll find this book an inspiration over the next 52 weeks. Our hope is that every week you will read, and put into practice, something that will help you shape your week and energize you – perhaps inspire you to do things differently – focus on the positive – or change your perspective – and to live a happier, healthier life.

C&&&&&&&&&&&&&&&&&&&

"The only way to discover
the limits of the possible
is to go beyond them
into the impossible."

Arthur C. Clarke

C&&&&&&&&&&&&&&&&&&&

1. Believe the Impossible

Anything is possible. Very often the only person to place limits on our success is ourselves. Sometimes you have to dream the impossible and then truly believe it in order to galvanize yourself to take the necessary steps to make it happen.

Here's a great quote to ponder on:

> "I can't believe that!" said Alice. "One can't believe impossible things."

> "I daresay you haven't had much practice," said the Queen. "When I was your age, I always did it for half-an-hour a day. Why, sometimes I've believed as many as six impossible things before breakfast."

> (Lewis Carroll, Through the Looking Glass)

There are two lessons here. Firstly, how crucial it is to take the time to think, dream and plan – you can't think creatively when you're rushed off your feet. Secondly, to think big – to embrace the impossible.

In the '80s I climbed Mount Kinabalu in Malaysia. This wasn't a mountain climb in terms of using ropes and crampons – but, rather, 13,500 exhausting feet of ascending rough steps that had been carved into the mountain. For me, who is not naturally athletic, this feat was impossible in itself, but half way up I was overtaken by a young man who was undertaking the record for RUNNING up the mountain. Not only that, but this man had prosthetic feet. He, truly, had dreamed the impossible – and achieved it.

Is there something you have long dreamed of doing, having or being, but others have told you it was impossible?

Could this be the year that you set out to achieve it?

❧❧❧❧❧❧❧❧❧❧❧❧❧❧

"Slow down and enjoy life. It's
not only the scenery you miss by
going too fast – you also miss the
sense of where you're going
and why."

Eddie Cantor

❧❧❧❧❧❧❧❧❧❧❧❧❧❧

2. Slow Down and Enjoy the Journey

As we ease our way into the New Year, there's one theme that seems to crop up again and again. People are feeling that their lives are spiralling out of control – the pace of life is just too fast and too relentless – and they're desperately wanting to find a way to SLOW DOWN.

This brings to mind a radio programme I heard once which included an interview with a man who still travelled the roads in his horse-drawn caravan. In fact, the interview was conducted on the caravan itself, accompanied by the evocative sound of the horse's hooves clip-clopping on the road. The man travelled the same route day after day and he was describing how he just couldn't understand the modern way, as he watched people hurtling past him in their cars, rushing from A to B as fast as they could.

In his words: "They just don't get the chance to go slow and enjoy what's around them. The countryside around here isn't special, but there's so much beauty to see in it when you take the time to look. I always say that it's not the getting there that's important. What's important is to enjoy the journey."

That's all very well for him, I hear you cry. What if you've got to earn a living or run a business; you've got bills to pay and children to ferry to swimming or football? I admit that few of us have the luxury of being able to take things at such a slow pace as the man in his gypsy caravan. But there's no doubt that taking time out to slow down and recharge your batteries – physically, mentally and spiritually – is absolutely vital. Not only will you feel revived, but you'll find that your productivity will increase dramatically as well.

So my challenge to you this week is to try to find a way – some-where, somehow – in your busy schedule to just SLOW DOWN and enjoy the journey.

ᘓᕘᕙᕘᕙᕘᕙᕚᕚᕚᕚᕚᕚᘍ

"In order to be utterly happy, the
only thing necessary is to refrain
from comparing this moment
with other moments in the past,
which I often did not fully enjoy
because I was comparing them
with other moments
of the future."

André Gide

ᘓᕘᕙᕘᕙᕘᕙᕚᕚᕚᕚᕚᕚᘍ

3. Treasure The Present

"Imagine a bank which credits your account each morning with £86,400. It does not carry a balance over from day to day, nor does it allow you to keep any cash balance and every evening cancels whatever part of the amount you have failed to use during the day. What would you do? Draw out every penny, of course!

Well, everybody has such a bank – its name is TIME. Every morning it credits you with 86,400 seconds. Every night it writes off as lost whatever of this you have failed to invest to good purpose.

> To realise the value of ONE YEAR ask a student who has failed a grade.
>
> To realise the value of ONE MONTH ask a mother who has given birth to a premature baby.
>
> To realise the value of ONE DAY ask an editor of a weekly newspaper.
>
> To realise the value of ONE MINUTE ask a person who has just missed a train.
>
> To realise the value of ONE SECOND ask a person who has avoided an accident.
>
> To realise the value of ONE MILLI-SECOND ask the person who has won a silver medal in the Olympics.
>
> Treasure every moment you have.
>
> Yesterday is history – Tomorrow is a mystery – Today is a gift.
>
> That is why it is called the PRESENT."
>
> (Author unknown)

Have a great week – 604,800 seconds and counting…!

☙ ⟶⟵ ❧

"Within you there is a stillness
and sanctuary to which you can retreat
at anytime and be yourself."

The Dhammapada

☙ ⟶⟵ ❧

4. Great Beginnings

How do you start your day? I know how easy it is to get straight out of bed and step right onto the hamster wheel – with barely enough time to grab a piece of toast and a quick cup of tea before you rush headlong into the day.

The way in which you start your day sets you up for what's ahead – and starting it well can make all the difference. I appreciate that if you have young children this tip might be a bit of a stretch – but see if there's still a way to carve out some 'me' time and get your day off to a great start after they have been attended to.

If you were to design the perfect start to your day, what would it look like? Would you …

- Take some time to meditate or do some yoga…

- Go out for a gentle stroll, listen to the bird song and take the time to rejoice in the things around you…

- Spend fifteen minutes reading an inspirational book, or listening to an inspirational recording…

- Go to the gym, or do some high-energy, aerobic exercise…

- Spend ten minutes doing absolutely nothing … allow yourself to daydream …

If you were to take the time – and make the conscious effort – to start your day off well, what difference do you think it would make?

"Men often become what they
believe themselves to be. If I
believe I cannot do something, it
makes me incapable of doing it.
But when I believe I can, then I
acquire the ability to do it even if
I didn't have it in the beginning."

Mahatma Gandhi

5. The Year of Living Boldly

A couple of months ago an acquaintance of mine – a woman in her 40s – made the decision to sell her house, pack up and move lock, stock and barrel from the north of England to the South Island of New Zealand. She's started a new business and a totally new life. In my book that's really bold!

I keep hearing personal stories from people who have given up secure, well-paid jobs in the corporate world and taken a leap of faith to steer their lives into a new direction. Many are taking the opportunity to follow their personal dream – and pursuing things that they've always wanted to do, but never before felt brave enough.

Could this be the year that you decide to make a bold move? Is it time for you to take steps towards doing something you've wanted to do for ages, but never felt brave enough? Is this your "year of living dangerously"?

If your heart says yes, but your head is holding you back, here's a tip that may help to put things into perspective: Project yourself forward to your 80th birthday and imagine that you're looking back over your life. From this vantage point, is there anything that you really wish you'd done but perhaps weren't brave enough at the time? In other words, can you look back over the span of your life and not have any regrets?

The key word here is 'regret'. Often people will say: I need to make this move now (even though it's scary) because I know that if I don't I'll regret it later. It's true. So – BE BOLD! And ask yourself this question: "If not now – when?"

⊂≈≈≈≈≈≈≈≈≈≈≈≈≈≈⊃

"The way to develop the
best that is in a person
is by appreciation and
encouragement."

Charles Schwab

⊂≈≈≈≈≈≈≈≈≈≈≈≈≈≈⊃

6. When In Doubt, Add Helium!

One of the most important ingredients in creating a successful life is remembering to appreciate others.

Imagine that every person is like a helium balloon, and the helium inside the balloon represents each person's self-confidence. When you add helium, the balloon expands and floats upwards. Take helium out and it deflates, drops to the ground and shrinks.

My challenge for the week is to make it a HABIT to consciously "add helium" to people's balloons... Find ways to say or do something to others which increases the amount of helium – or self confidence – that they've got. Something that makes them feel good, feel special, feel appreciated. It could be a friend, employee, a client, family, your bank manager, the person at the check-out in Tesco – even the person who cuts in front of you in their car.

Why is this important?:

- Good will spreads. Think of the impact it could have in terms of increasing the sum of happiness and potential in the world if everyone adopted this attitude.

- It feels great to boost someone else's confidence.

- It makes you an extremely 'attractive' person.

- People will be drawn to you.

- Your own self-confidence will increase as a result.

CR⧸⧸⧸⧸⧸⧸⧸⧸⧸⧸⧸⧸⧸BO

"Undoubtedly, we become
what we envisage."

Claude M. Bristol

CR⧸⧸⧸⧸⧸⧸⧸⧸⧸⧸⧸⧸⧸BO

7. Writing Your Obituary

In 2005 Roz Savage became the first solo woman to compete in the Atlantic Rowing Race. She set out from the Canaries to row 3,000 miles across the Atlantic Ocean, alone and unsupported, and eventually arrived in Antigua on 13th March 2006 after 103 days alone at sea.

What really intrigued me about her story was the process which had led to her embarking on this extraordinary adventure. After leaving University she had followed a typical career path – working her way up the corporate ladder, firstly as a Management Consultant and then moving on to be an Investment Banker in the City of London. So far so good, but eleven years later, when she was in her early 30s, she started to get a niggling feeling that something was missing and that perhaps there was "more to life than this..."

 The turning point came when she sat down one day and wrote two versions of her own obituary. The first version related to her current life, while the second described a life that was a very different story! It contained words that were full of meaning and vibrancy for her – 'adventurous', 'courageous', 'fearless' and 'colourful' – and that was the point at which she decided to make changes to her life so that it more closely resembled the life she wanted to live and, ultimately, how she wanted to be remembered.

How about you? What would your obituary say about you? Is this how you want to be remembered? Writing your own obituary may seem a touch morbid, but there's no doubt that it's a powerful way of focusing the mind on what's really important to you and how you want to live your life.

಼಼಼಼಼಼಼಼಼಼಼಼಼಼

"Come to the edge," he said.

They said, "We are afraid."

"Come to the edge," he said.

They came. He pushed them …

and they flew."

Guillaume Appollinaire

಼಼಼಼಼಼಼಼಼಼಼಼಼಼

8. There's No Such Thing as a 'Wrong' Decision

For all those who have a hard time making decisions – this is for you:

In her excellent book, "Feel the Fear and Do It Anyway", Susan Jeffers points out that when we have a decision to make, we tend to look at it in terms of making either a 'right' choice or a 'wrong' choice. As a result, we find ourselves paralysed by being too scared of making the wrong decision.

Her suggestion is that we change our perspective and consider BOTH choices as being right. No matter what happens, whichever decision you make, it won't be wrong – it will simply result in a different outcome. Either way, there will be new things to learn, new people to meet, new opportunities will open up, and so on.

She calls it the 'No-Lose Model' and this perspective can really open one up to the possibilities of choices – rather than feeling restricted by them.

I know the feeling of being paralysed by indecision only too well. Several years ago I was absolutely incapable of making a decision as to whether or not to end a long-term relationship. Without the benefit of a crystal ball, I was so scared of making the 'wrong' decision that I literally couldn't move. In the end I did make the choice to end the relationship, and within three months had met the wonderful man that I now share my life with.

The point is, that even if I hadn't experienced this admittedly fairy-tale ending, I know that lots of other opportunities would have come my way, and – as Jeffers emphasises – I WOULD have been able to deal with any of them.

CR◅◈◅◈◅◈◅◈◈◈◈◈◈◈BO

"When we truly care for
ourselves it becomes possible
to care more profoundly
about other people."

Edith Le Shen

CR◅◈◅◈◅◈◅◈◈◈◈◈◈◈BO

9. Do Something Fabulous

I was talking with a friend recently and she happened to mention that one of her personal goals this year was "to do something fabulous" each and every month. True to her word, in a couple of days she was off to spend a long weekend at a luxury health spa in Budapest!

What a GREAT idea!

Intrigued by this concept I asked assorted friends and family what they would do if they were going to do "something fabulous" and the responses just illustrate what wonderfully diverse beings we are...

- Buy and plant a beautiful tree

- A weekend break in Venice

- A hot air balloon trip

- Take the family for a picnic in the countryside

- Walk the Thames Path

- Take a helicopter ride

- Book a weekend retreat

- Indulge in a reflexology session

If you were to do something fabulous this month, what would it be? And why restrict it to once a month? You could make it once a week – or even daily ...

Whatever you choose, have a fabulous week!

CR◈◈◈◈◈◈◈◈◈◈◈◈◈◈◈BO

"Take the first step in faith.
You don't have to see
the whole staircase,
just take the first step."

Martin Luther King

CR◈◈◈◈◈◈◈◈◈◈◈◈◈◈◈BO

10. Single Daily Action

If you are trying to reach a specific goal, or want to embark on a project but are having trouble getting started or motivated, a good strategy is to take action towards it on a daily basis.

No matter how small or simple it is, some action is better than none, and soon you will start to gather momentum and begin to rocket towards reaching your target.

Some examples might be:

> Your goal is to improve your health and fitness: you could choose to use the stairs at work instead of the lift or make a point of drinking 8 glasses of water every day.

> Your goal is to write a novel or short story: you might choose to write just one paragraph or page a day.

The most important thing is to GET INTO ACTION. Not only will you feel much more positive, you will soon start to see the results. Why not try this for the next week and see what happens.

- What is/are your goal(s)?

- What will your Single Daily Action(s) be?

Here's to an extraordinarily productive week!

CR∿∾∿∾∿∾∾∾∾∾∾∾∾BO

"If it doesn't absorb you,
if it isn't any fun,
don't do it."

D.H. Lawrence

CR∿∾∿∾∿∾∾∾∾∾∾∾∾BO

11. Beware the 'Shoulds'

This tip may seem simple, but it is extremely powerful, and shows how changing just one word can have a profound impact on your life.

How often do you use the word 'should'?

The things that we love to do – that are in line with who we are and our values – are never 'shoulds'. They are the things that we look forward to and which give us energy.

'Shoulds', on the other hand, are usually energy drainers.

Whenever we say something like "I really should do ...." it implies that it's something that we don't really want to do – or that perhaps we feel someone else wants us to do. It also implies that we don't have a lot of choice in the matter.

Next time you catch yourself – or someone else – using the word 'should', try replacing it with 'COULD' instead. This immediately gives you the element of choice. It's not something you've got to do, it's something you can choose to do – or not. It's up to you.

Feels a lot better, doesn't it?

附曉曉曉曉曉曉曉曉曉

"If you never say 'no' then what
is your 'yes' worth?"

(Anon)

附曉曉曉曉曉曉曉曉曉

12. Say YES to You...

There's one issue that crops up over and over again in coaching sessions and that's the need to say 'No' more often. Such a tiny word. Seemingly so insignificant. But one that has such far-reaching implications.

It doesn't matter whether you're trying to improve the way you manage your time, your work/life balance, or your self-confidence, I guarantee that learning to say 'No' will make a massive difference.

It's so much easier to say 'Yes' to things. We may feel flattered to be asked – saying 'No' might mean you're not a team player – perhaps we don't want to let someone down or hurt their feelings – and of course we want to feel liked and included. But remember: Each time you say 'Yes' to one thing, you are effectively saying 'No' to something else. And that may very well be time that you would otherwise have spent with your family, friends or – crucially – time for yourself.

How to do it? I think one of the best tips is to play for time. Whenever someone asks you to commit to doing something, don't say "yes" as an automatic response. Instead, tell them that you'll let them know in an hour – or tomorrow – or next week. This way you get the chance to think it over and decide if you really do have time to do it – and/or if it's something that you can say yes to wholeheartedly. (see also Tip 28)

If you want to measure the relative merits of those claims on your time, just try this mental exercise:

By saying YES to .... ,

I am saying NO to ....

Saying 'No' to the things that don't truly serve you means that you are saying a resounding 'Yes' to yourself.

"Man's mind stretched to a
new idea never goes back to its
original shape."

Oliver Wendell Holmes

13. Brainstorming

Definition of brainstorm: A spontaneous group discussion to produce ideas and ways of solving problems.

(New Oxford Dictionary of English)

I love brainstorming! Let's say you are facing a particular challenge, or you have the seeds of an idea in your head or you want to generate lots of ideas and strategies. Rather than sitting in splendid isolation with a pen and piece of paper, it can be infinitely more productive (and more enjoyable) to gather several friends and /or colleagues and brainstorm together.

Elect a note taker – or turn on a tape recorder so that no ideas or comments are lost. Ask people to think out of the box – and NEVER discard an idea, even if at first it seems totally impracticable.

Once you've got a list of ideas and suggestions, take each one in turn – even the most 'off the wall' ones – and ask these four questions:

1. What is the useful element in this idea?
2. What are the problematic aspects of this idea?
3. How can I get around the impractical elements of this idea?
4. What further ideas does this idea inspire?

The key point here is that even though an idea might seem fraught with difficulties, don't discard it. It's quite possible that – on closer examination – another workable idea can come from it.

CR✿✿✿✿✿✿✿✿✿✿✿✿✿✿BO

"Action springs not
from thought, but from a
readiness for responsibility."

Dietrich Bonhoffer

CR✿✿✿✿✿✿✿✿✿✿✿✿✿✿BO

14. The Three Frogs

Question: Three frogs are sitting on a water-lily leaf. Two decide to jump. How many are left?

Answer: Three. It's not enough simply to decide to jump; you've actually got to do it!

This may be an old riddle, but it's a good reminder that thinking or dreaming about doing something isn't enough – you've got to get into action as well.

After what has seemed like a very long winter, the days are at last becoming longer and a little warmer, the natural world is getting on with its cycle of growth and activity, and this Tip is all about shaking off the heavy mantle of winter and starting to grow.

Is there anything that you've been thinking about doing – or a dream or goal that may have lain dormant over winter? Do you now feel ready to jump off the lily pad and into the pond? Are you ready to make a big splash? If so, ask yourself, what's the first step I need to take? Once you're clear on that – just do it.

If you're not ready to start moving towards a major goal or dream, here's a nice, gentle way to get into action. It's one of my favourite exercises for those moments when you're feeling a bit lethargic, stuck, or unproductive:

Ten Tiny Changes: List ten changes you'd like to make for yourself. Write a list with each item starting

"I would like to ...."

Think of all the things that have lain dormant over the winter months – things that you've been putting off until you had more energy – things that will really make a difference and make you feel good. Aim to cross at least one of those things off your list this week.

"Cats seem to go on the principle
that it never does any harm
to ask for what you want"

Joseph Wood Krutch

15. Defining Boundaries

I recently spotted a sign at the entrance to a building site. Clearly intended for those working on the site, its message couldn't have been simpler:

NO HAT

NO BOOTS

NO JOB!

I found myself thinking, if only we could be as clear, concise and straightforward in our approach to relationships how much easier things would be. As a general rule, we seem to find it hard to state clearly what our needs are, and more specifically, what behaviour we consider to be acceptable from others and what behaviour isn't. So often, we skirt around the issue, dropping hints here and there and hoping that the other person will catch on.

Establishing strong boundaries around what is and isn't acceptable from others is extremely important for successful, healthy relationships. Boundaries are like an imaginary line of protection that you draw around you. Examples of people overstepping your boundaries might be: your spouse criticising you in front of others; unthinking friends who call you late at night when you're getting ready for bed; a co-worker who makes a habit of shedding their workload onto you.

So what can we do about this? The first step is to become clear in your own mind about what behaviour is acceptable to you and what isn't.

Then you will need to communicate this to those around you. This needn't be done in an angry or proscriptive way. All you are doing, in effect, is making clear to others that you respect yourself and you ask that they respect you, too.

Pro rata, you could invite them to let you know if there are any ways in which you are overstepping their boundaries – and take steps to modify your behaviour accordingly.

❦❦❦❦❦❦❦❦❦❦❦❦❦❦

"The key is not to
prioritise your schedule,
but to schedule your priorities."

Stephen Covey

❦❦❦❦❦❦❦❦❦❦❦❦❦❦

16. Rocks, Gravel and Sand

In his book "First Things First" Stephen Covey describes a lecture he attended on the topic of 'time'. The lecturer took a large glass jar and set it down on a table with some small rocks beside it. He placed the rocks in the jar and asked the audience whether they thought the jar was full.

Everybody laughed and replied that yes, it was full. Then the lecturer reached under the table and pulled out a container of gravel. He poured in the gravel and shook the jar so that the gravel filled the spaces that had been left by the rocks. Again he asked the audience if the jar was full. By this time they had cottoned on, and replied no.

'Good!' he replied. And he reached under the table and repeated the process, only this time with sand, which went into the spaces left by the rocks and the gravel. Then he asked what had been the point of the demonstration.

Somebody said, 'Well, there are gaps, and if you really work at it, you can always fit more into your life.'

'No,' he said, 'that's not the point. The point is this: if you hadn't put these big rocks in first, would you ever have gotten any of them in?'

If we relate this illustration to our lives, the 'rocks' are representative of the things that are really important to us. The gravel represents the other things in life that matter, but on a smaller scale. The sand is everything else. The small stuff. If we put the sand and gravel into the jar first, there's no room for the rocks.

As Covey says, take care of the rocks first – the things that really matter. Set your priorities. The rest is just gravel and sand.

ભ—₰₰₰₰₰₰₰₰₰₰₰—ᐁ

"The secret of getting ahead
is getting started.

The secret of getting started
is breaking your complex,
overwhelming tasks into
small
manageable
tasks and then
starting on the first one."

Mark Twain

ભ—₰₰₰₰₰₰₰₰₰₰₰—ᐁ

17. Procrastination

Over the years I've come across some really cracking examples of procrastination. I recall my sister telling me about a friend of hers – an eminent academic – who confessed she'd chosen to remove the accumulated grease from the back of her cooker with a teaspoon rather than start work on an article for an academic journal.

A colleague of mine finally finished reading "The Procrastinator's Handbook", having admitted taking it back to the library three times to renew it!

For those of us for whom these examples sound all too familiar, here are a few tips to help beat the demon of procrastination:

1. Ask yourself: "If this task is something I keep putting off, is it something I need to do at all? Can I shelve it completely? Is it no longer relevant to my life? Could I delegate it?" If not, just do it.

2. Sometimes a task can seem so immense and overwhelming that it literally paralyses us. Break the task down and ask yourself "what's the one thing I need to do to get started?" It may be to turn the computer on; write the first sentence; make the first call. Whatever it is, just do it.

3. Give yourself a short time limit to work on the task. Time Management Coach, Mark Forster, suggests setting a kitchen timer for, say, 10-15 minutes and ONLY working on the task for that amount of time. You'll be amazed at how well this technique works.

4. Do it first. Whatever you're putting off, do it first otherwise it will slip to the bottom of the list and most probably stay there to be superseded by other, less important tasks.

"Too often we underestimate the power of a touch, a smile, a kind word, a listening ear, an honest compliment, or the smallest act of caring, all of which have the potential to turn a life around."

Leo Buscaglia

18. The Butterfly Effect

Many of you will be familiar with this theory. The scientists among you will no doubt correct me here, but I believe the idea behind it is that a butterfly fluttering its wings in one part of the world can have an impact on the climate in another part of the world.

It struck me that in a small way – like a single butterfly – each one of us has the capacity to influence hundreds – even thousands – of people through the way that we behave.

Here's an example. There's a particularly nasty road junction in my village, where you can wait for ages for a gap in the endless stream of traffic. When I can, I'll stop to create the space and the opportunity for people to pull out.

The point is, I've noticed time after time, that the driver I stopped for will invariably do the same for someone else. Who knows – perhaps they then do the same for another driver. And so it goes on.

A few years ago, my partner and I broke down on the motorway in France on our way home to catch the ferry. Another motorist noticed us at the side of the road, with our radiator spewing steam, and pulled in behind us. He went to the boot of his car, pulled out a container of water and handed it to us. No, he didn't need it back – we could keep it and fill it up as we drove on. That random act of kindness not only got us to the ferry on time, it had a profound impact on both of us. Ever since then, we've always stopped to help when we see someone in trouble on the road.

Random acts of kindness. Who knows the impact they can have.

ଔଈଌଈଌଈଌଈଈଈଈ

"The maxim
'nothing avails but perfection'
may be spelled 'paralysis'.""

Winston Churchill

ଔଈଌଈଌଈଌଈଈଈଈ

19. Perfectly Imperfect

For as long as I can remember I've wanted to do things 'perfectly' and it's an absolute nightmare. Not only are you far more likely to procrastinate – but at its worst it can actually paralyse you because of the fear that whatever you do 'it won't be good enough.'

I was talking with some new coaches this week, and we were discussing putting together relevant materials to welcome a new client. Some of them were feeling quite anxious about this and worrying about what to include in their welcome packs.

The point was made that these materials don't have to be 'perfect' – just get something together, make it as good as you possibly can for now, and you can always improve them later. The collective sigh was audible! As someone put it: "That's great – permission to be perfectly imperfect!"

Perfectionism can paralyse. The truth is that we're NOT perfect. We will do the very best we can, at the time, and with the resources available to us. So my tip for this week is to give yourself a break and allow yourself to be Perfectly Imperfect. OK, what you produce may not be 100%, but in most cases you will have the opportunity to improve on it later. Or, as William Shakespeare aptly put it 400 years ago: "Striving to better, oft we mar what's well."

"The man least dependant upon
the morrow goes to meet the
morrow most cheerfully."

Epicurus

20. What's Your Theme?

Every now and again I will ask my clients to identify a 'theme' for themselves – something they would like to focus their attention on in the weeks to come.

The key is to choose a theme that will inspire you to think more positively about something – or help you to focus on changes you would like to make.

Here are some real examples of themes that people have chosen:

"Put myself first"

"If it isn't fun, don't do it!"

"Look smart"

"Delegate, delegate, delegate"

"Leave early for all appointments"

"Live in the moment"

What would you like your theme to be for the next week?

Choose something that you'd like to focus on in the next seven days that will really make a difference to your life. Write your theme on post-its and scatter them strategically around your home or office – where you will notice them frequently.

When our heads are all too often crammed with mental 'to do' lists, this exercise can really help to act as a conscious reminder to focus on something positive.

""Often people attempt to live
their lives backwards: they try
to have more things, or more
money, in order to do more
of what they want so that
they will be happier.

The way it actually works is the
reverse. You must first be who
you really are, then do what you
need to do, in order to have
what you want."

Margaret Young

21. The Soldier and the Priest

I once heard this story about a priest, who was confronted by a soldier while he was walking down a road in pre-revolutionary Russia. The soldier, aiming his rifle at the priest, commanded, 'Who are you? Where are you going? Why are you going there?'

Unfazed, the priest calmly replied, 'How much do they pay you?'

Somewhat surprised, the soldier responded, 'Twenty-five kopecks a month.'

The priest paused, and in a deeply thoughtful manner said, 'I have a proposal for you. I'll pay you fifty kopecks each month if you stop me here every day and challenge me to respond to those same three questions.'

(Taken from Leadership From the Inside Out by Kevin Cashman)

CR⋅⋅⋅⋅⋅⋅⋅⋅⋅⋅⋅⋅BO

This is such a good story. The questions seem simple enough, but of course, they require considerable thought and a deep examination of your future direction.

How would YOU respond to those same three questions?

- Who are you?

- Where are you going?

- Why are you going there?

ରେ ଏକ ଏକ ଏକ ଏକ ଏକ ଏକ

"May I treat others as I would
be treated. What I like not for
myself may I dispense not to
others."

A Sufi prayer

ରେ ଏକ ଏକ ଏକ ଏକ ଏକ ଏକ

22. Verbal Paper Cuts

Paper cuts are those irritating, superficial cuts that you can get from mishandling paper. Little blood is lost, but they can be painful for several days.

The paper cut is a useful metaphor for relationships. Has anyone ever made a 'cutting' comment to you that seemed superficial on the surface, but that caused you considerable discomfort? Have YOU ever said unkind words to someone else? Your intent was probably not to hurt them – but the result of unkind words, even if spoken in jest, can be like the sting of a paper cut.

If you'd like to get rid of 'verbal paper cuts' in a relationship here are a few suggestions:

1. Firstly, just become aware of what it feels like to give or receive a verbal paper cut.

2. Ask those close to you to give you honest feedback. Make a clear agreement with those close to you to let you know when you've made a hurtful remark. Agree that you'll do the same if they say something hurtful to you.

3. When a 'verbal paper cut' is made by anyone, ask the questions, "What was the reason I said those things? Is there some unspoken resentment there that I haven't dealt with? Was I being funny at someone else's expense?"

4. Finally, take steps to deal with the anger or resentment in a conscious and constructive fashion.

(Based on an article by Bernice Ross and Byron Van Arsdale)

CR⤸⤸⤸⤸⤸⤸⤸⤸⤸⤸⤸⤸⤸BO

"Look to your health; and if you
have it, praise God, and value it
next to a good conscience; for
health is the second blessing we
mortals are capable of;
a blessing that money
cannot buy."

Izaak Walton

CR⤸⤸⤸⤸⤸⤸⤸⤸⤸⤸⤸⤸⤸BO

23. Just One Change…

A few months ago I attended a talk about taking care of yourself – specifically looking after your health. The one thing that I took away from the talk was the insistence of the speaker that we should make just one change each day towards becoming healthier.

Personally, I'm not naturally attracted to exercise – in fact most of the time I'm downright lazy – but I was determined to take her advice and somehow take steps to improve my level of fitness. And so, in a rash moment, I made a commitment to walk a short circuit near my home which includes a very steep hill.

The first time it took nearly 20 minutes. A month later I clocked it at just under fourteen. By doing this daily I'd knocked over five minutes off my time. The point is that this exercise takes less than 20 minutes per day and it's already having a hugely beneficial effect. I feel much better – I have more energy – it's a great way to start each day – even my skin looks better!

What change would you be willing to make – daily – to improve your health and fitness? It could be something really simple, like choosing to get off the bus one stop sooner and walking the last part to work. Perhaps you will renew that lapsed gym membership? Or actually USE the membership you're paying for! Maybe you could walk round the block at lunchtime instead of eating at your desk?

To sharpen your resolve – and help you to keep to the commitment – tell someone else (family, friends, work colleagues, your coach) what you plan to do and ask them to keep you accountable.

It doesn't have to be a huge change. It just needs to be something.

❦❧

"To choose time is to save time."

Francis Bacon

24. Who Knows Where the Time Goes...

Time is fast becoming one of the most precious commodities of the 21st Century – yet if I was to ask you to describe how you spend your time, would you be able to tell me?

Everyone complains of being 'too busy' but what exactly are we all doing? How are we choosing to spend our precious time? In the past couple of weeks I've found myself getting to the end of the working day and wondering what on earth I've been so busy doing all day. Am I using my time wisely? Am I being productive? Are my activities moving me towards what I want to achieve and what I hold to be important?

If you find yourself asking the same kinds of questions, here's an exercise which will hopefully give you some answers:

For the next week try keeping a TIME LOG. Keep as accurate and detailed a record as you can of everything you do each day. Then at the end of each day – and the week – do an analysis of where your time goes.

I often ask clients to do this and the results can be a real eye-opener. The first time I tried it I was shocked to discover that I was spending 2-3 hours each day just on emails and, even worse, that I was typically working 10-12 hour days. Well that had to stop! The thing was, that until I did the Time Log and saw it in black and white I honestly didn't realise how much time I was wasting.

Once you know exactly where your time goes, you will be in a far better position to take control and make some clear choices.

CR ᗷᗷᗷᗷᗷᗷᗷᗷᗷᗷᗷᗷᗷ BO

"Nobody can make you feel
inferior without your consent."

Eleanor Roosevelt

CR ᗷᗷᗷᗷᗷᗷᗷᗷᗷᗷᗷᗷᗷ BO

25. Quick Confidence Booster

It doesn't matter how positive, upbeat or confident you are as a person, there are going to be times when you feel quite the opposite. This can often be the result of someone saying or doing something that knocks your confidence and makes you doubt your abilities. Sometimes there doesn't even have to be a specific reason – we just 'get the blues' – nothing seems to go right – and our confidence falters.

So what's the best way to deal with this? Over the years, I've found that one of the quickest remedies is to have something handy that serves as a reminder of how great you really are. I often advise my clients to start collecting things that make them feel good – and that remind them of all their special qualities, unique abilities and talents. It could be a loving or encouraging letter that someone has sent you – or an uplifting card or email. Or perhaps a photo which recalls a time when you were feeling on top of the world.

Keep these reminders in a box, file or drawer (or a special folder on the computer) and whenever you're feeling a bit down, simply reach for it and read the contents. I have a 'Feel Good Folder' which sits by the side of my desk – labelled "in case of emergency open and read immediately!" One of my clients has a collage on her wall – pictures, photos, phrases, words, inspiring quotes – a gallery of all the people who love her and think she's wonderful.

It's remarkable how easy it is to forget all the positives – and especially so when you're feeling a bit down. These reminders will go a long way towards restoring your confidence and sense of well-being.

"Yesterday is not ours to recover,
but tomorrow is ours
to win or lose."

Lyndon B Johnson

26. Reflections

It's hard to believe that we're more than half way through the year. With summer upon us, and many people getting ready to go on holiday, this is a great time to reflect on what you have achieved in the first half of the year, and also how you would like the next five months to look.

Step One:

Think about all of your achievements so far this year – note them all, either in your mind or on paper. Make it as long a list as you can and then give yourself a real or imaginary pat on the back for everything – no matter how small – that you have achieved.

Step Two:

Consider the rest of the year. How would you like your life to be different by the end of this year? Another way to look at this is to project yourself forward to December 31st and look back over the last 5 months. What would have to have happened for you to feel thoroughly contented with the way this year has progressed?

Step Three:

Make a list of three key things that you would like to achieve by the end of the year. Is there a new and different challenge you'd like to set yourself? Is there something you've been wanting to do for ages, but you keep putting it off? Why not include something outrageous or unexpected on your list?

Note: this is a really good exercise to do at the end of the year as well.

"Life is not the way it's supposed
to be. It's the way it is. The way
you cope with it is what
makes the difference."

Virginia Satir

27. Clearing the Decks

Have you ever been in a situation where you've taken so much on that you feel completely swamped and don't know where to start?

If this feels familiar, here's a tip that might help you to take back control:

1. Make a list of ALL the things you're currently doing – all the activities, projects, hobbies etc.

2. Mentally 'clear the decks' – in other words, assume that you no longer have to do any of these things. Your diary is totally empty – your time is 100% your own.

3. Then CHOOSE those activities that you want to put back on the list. Think very carefully. Be ruthless. Be highly selective.

Be sure that you only put back those activities that you feel genuinely enthusiastic about. Examine carefully those things you think you should or ought to do (see Tip 11).

There may be some things you feel you have to put back, but wish you didn't. Listen carefully to that and ask yourself: "Are these activities ones that I might want to drop or to delegate?"

Clearing the Decks is a great way to eliminate 'shoulds' and to help you make conscious choices about how you want to spend your precious time.

CR&~&~&~&~&~&~&~&~BO

"Saying no can be the
ultimate self-care."

Claudia Black

CR&~&~&~&~&~&~&~&~BO

28. The Hamburger Response

Regular Tips readers will know that one of my 'hot topics' is the importance of learning how to say "no" (see Tip No. 12). I believe it's a crucial life skill – not to mention one of the key weapons needed in the battle to achieve that elusive nirvana – Work/Life Balance.

How often have you said 'yes' to something and immediately regretted it? Perhaps your diary was already jammed and you really didn't have time to add that extra networking meeting or social commitment.

I've found that saying 'no' is a lot easier if you have this simple formula to follow: Picture a hamburger … think of the two buns as representing positive statements and the burger a negative one. The idea is to 'wrap' your negative statement in between two positive ones in order to soften the impact. It really works. Here's an example:

A colleague has called and asked if you would be on the committee for a new project he's launching. You know full well that you don't have time to get involved, and that it's not of any interest to you personally or professionally. So, what do you say?

"I really appreciate your inviting me to be part of your project." (positive)

"I'm really sorry, but for the next few months my schedule is absolutely crammed and I don't have any spare time, so I'm unable to accept". (negative)

"But thanks for thinking of me – and I wish you the very best of luck with the project."

You've just said no, but in a very respectful way. Obviously you'll need to couch your refusal in the kind of language that feels comfortable for you – but hopefully using the "hamburger response" will make you feel more comfortable about saying 'No' when you need to.

"Your own resolution to succeed
is more important than any
other one thing."

Abraham Lincoln

29. The Meaning of Success

Just before he died, John Lennon recorded his first album for many years. I heard a track from the album recently and while it might not be the most inspiring song he ever wrote, the words really got me thinking. The song is called 'Woman' (written for his wife) and the first verse includes these lines:

> …Woman, I will try express,
> My inner feelings and thankfulness,
> For showing me the meaning of success…

It's that last line that gave me pause. Here was a man had fame and fortune by the bucket-load. But, at the time he wrote these lyrics he had turned his back on his his hell-raising days and on his celebrity lifestyle, and had spent the past few years at home with his wife, baking bread and looking after his young son.

The implication I draw from these lyrics is that for John Lennon, the true meaning of success was not in the obvious trappings of wealth and fame, but rather, finding peace in a simple life of love and harmony with his wife and son.

Ironically, there are those who seem to have all the external trappings of success – lots of money, great job, happy family – but inside they're absolutely miserable. Their seemingly happy life is totally incongruent with who they are and what's truly important to them.

So, what's YOUR definition of success? This is a question I often ask my clients, and it is fundamental to the coaching process. Of course, everyone's definition will be unique to them. There's no right or wrong – only what's right for you.

The common thread, though, is that once we are clear about what 'success' means for us, it's much easier to act with certainty. It also gives us a solid base – a yardstick – from which to make decisions about the future.

❧❧❧❧❧❧❧❧❧❧❧❧❧❧

"Everything changes
when you change."

Jim Rohn

❧❧❧❧❧❧❧❧❧❧❧❧❧❧

30. Tolerations

What are you 'tolerating' in your life? In other words, what are you putting up with? And how much is that draining your energy?

'Tolerations' are those things that irritate and frustrate you – they make you sigh each time you think of them – your heart sinks and you can almost feel the energy being sapped from you. You know you need to sort them out, but somehow they keep being dropped to the bottom of the 'to do' list. Tolerations could be:

- the button that needs sewing onto your favourite shirt
- filthy car
- cluttered desk
- broken microwave
- front door that needs painting
- overdue letter or conversation

They may seem insignificant, but even the smallest things can build up to the point where they have an adverse impact on our energy levels. So it's important to become aware of 'tolerations' and eliminate them on a regular basis. Here's how to do it:

Step One:
Make a list of everything in your life that you're currently tolerating – big and small.

Step Two:
Pick FIVE and handle them in the next week – just get rid of them – in whatever way you choose.

Step Three:
Keep working through the list until all the items have been eliminated. It will make a huge difference, and will free up lots of energy for more positive pursuits.

Note: Repeat this exercise every 3-4 months.

CR෴෴෴෴෴෴෴෴෴෴෴෴෴BO

"If the only prayer you say in
your whole life is 'thank you'
that would suffice."

Meister Eckhart

CR෴෴෴෴෴෴෴෴෴෴෴෴෴BO

31. Gratitude

At certain times – particularly when life is throwing a series of ugly challenges at you – it can be very easy to dwell on all the problems, difficulties and negatives and to forget – or take for granted – those aspects of our lives which are working well for us.

Here are a couple of tips to keep you focused on the positives:

1. Make a list of at least 20 things you currently feel thankful for. This may take some thought, but if you persist you'll be surprised at what you can come up with. If certain people appear on your list you may want to let them know.

2. A Daily "Gratitude Journal": Some people find it inspiring to sit down at the end of each day and write down all the things they are feeling grateful for.

3. When author Jinny Ditzler (author of "Your Best Year Yet") and her husband were going through a rough time, they used to get together one night a week, open a bottle of wine and take turns making toasts for the best things that had happened the previous week. She writes: "even in the worst weeks, there are those little miracles and things to be grateful for. It makes such a difference to remember to focus on how lucky we are rather than on what a struggle it all is."

You'll be surprised at the impact 'focusing on the positives' can have to your attitude and sense of well-being.

CR👍👍👍👍👍👍👍👍👍👍👍👍👍👍BO

"Only dull people are
brilliant at breakfast!"

Oscar Wilde

CR👍👍👍👍👍👍👍👍👍👍👍👍👍👍BO

32. Natural Energy Cycles

We all have different 'natural energy cycles' – in other words, times of the day when our energy is naturally high or low.

I'm a 'morning' person, whereas I know people who do their best creative work burning the midnight oil. I've learned to recognise now when my energy is low and I consciously use those times for activities that don't require a lot of physical or mental effort.

When are you at your best? What times of day do you feel bright, clear-headed, full of energy? And when do you typically feel sluggish, fuzzy, tired?

Start to recognise these times and consciously use the times when you have most energy for those tasks that require more mental effort. The 'down' times are best utilised for more routine activities.

This is often easier said than done, but once you become more aware of this you can try to match the different tasks to the available energy levels, and build these in as part of your routine.

০৪৯৵৵৵৵৵৵৵৵৵৵৵৵৵৵৵৵৵০

"Much unhappiness has come
into the world because of
bewilderment and things
left unsaid."

Dostoevsky

০৪৯৵৵৵৵৵৵৵৵৵৵৵৵৵৵৵৵৵০

33. When in Doubt, Communicate!

Are you afraid to communicate what you really feel for fear of making waves, or hurting someone else? Sometimes it feels 'easier' not to say anything at all rather than face a potentially difficult discussion. The problem then, of course, is that the longer things go unsaid, the greater the likelihood of misunderstanding.

In the 90's the band REM broke up because, in the words of one of the members, they had become 'hopelessly estranged and terminally uncommunicative'.

Eventually they pulled themselves around and got back together. How did they do it? To quote Michael Stipe, the lead singer, "We talked. We just sat down and talked."

This sounds ludicrously simple – but it really can be just that simple. Communication can almost always resolve a problem. It just takes determination on everyone's part to sort it out and a total commitment to speak the truth. It's not always easy, but the following pointers should help:

1. Make it very safe for each person to communicate what needs to be said. Even though what the other person is saying may be hard for you to hear, don't get defensive and leap down their throat.

2. Listen and try to hear each other's point of view, and to understand it as they see it, rather than filtering it through your own experience. You may not agree with it, but it IS real for them.

3. Be sure to acknowledge what the other person has said even though you may not agree with it. Feeling heard is vital. Just a comment like "I can understand that" or "I see what you mean" is all it takes for the other person to feel heard and understood.

"How many people on their
deathbed wish they'd spent
more time at the office?"

Stephen Covey

34. Priorities

Sometimes we can get so caught up in the whirlpool of day-to-day living that we lose sight of those things we truly love to do; those things that are intrinsically 'us', that we feel passionate about, that make us naturally happy – content – excited – full of energy.

To re-connect with what some of these things might be, get yourself a pen and a piece of paper and then ask yourself this question:

> "If money were not a consideration, how would I choose to spend my time?"

Write down the first ten things that come to mind...

How many of these things are you doing on a regular basis?

Clearly, I'm not suggesting that making a living is not important – or that you give up your work. What I AM suggesting is that if you feel you've lost sight of what you really love to do – then perhaps some re-prioritising might be in order.

What will you have to do differently in order to make room for some or all of the things on your list?

"Though we travel the world
over to find the beautiful,
we must carry it within us,
or we find it not."

Ralph Waldo Emerson

35. Soft Time

A few evenings ago I was wandering back home from our allotment, having spent a peaceful quarter of an hour watering the lettuces, peas, carrots and runner beans. It was about 8pm – the air was warm and balmy – the swallows and swifts weaved, glided and dipped in the pink evening sky and as I walked down the hill, swinging my empty watering can, I was overcome by a sense of well-being. I felt completely content and at peace. I wasn't doing anything much, I wasn't achieving anything much, I was just taking my time – just being and enjoying the moment.

Spiritual writer and teacher Gill Edwards describes this kind of experience as 'Soft Time'. Soft Time embodies those moments or periods of time when you are completely wrapped up in what you are doing and enter a different, almost timeless world. As she puts it in her book 'Pure Bliss' they are "intensely creative and fulfilling periods when everything seems to flow ... blissful periods of simply relaxing and being-in-the-moment..."

In the hectic life we all seem to lead – with endless 'to do' lists, terrifyingly packed schedules, looming deadlines and multi-tasking (all characterised as living in Hard Time) it seems to me that "Soft Time" is becoming increasingly precious.

What constitutes 'soft time' for you? Is it gazing at a wonderful painting or sculpture? Exploring rock pools or looking for seashells? Luxuriating in a delicious aromatherapy bath? Or being utterly absorbed in a good book? When was the last time you enjoyed some 'soft time'? To quote Gill Edwards again, "When we live in Soft Time we feel more present and alive. We tap into our inner wisdom with ease. We are more focused and creative and perform at our peak... Living in Soft Time also releases our true potential..."

Sounds great, doesn't it? Whatever you do, don't let Soft Time become an added pressure, but, rather, be aware of the need to make space for it if you can. My guess is that even a few moments will nourish you immensely.

CR∽ର∾ର∽ର∾ର∽ର∾ର∽ର∾ର∽ର∽BO

"Invent your world. Surround
yourself with people, colour,
sounds and work that
nourish you."

Sark

CR∽ର∾ର∽ର∾ର∽ର∾ର∽ର∾ର∽ର∽BO

36. Success Teams

Whatever you want to achieve in your life – either on a personal or professional level – there's nothing like having a positive support team behind you, encouraging you at every turn; keeping you on track and picking you up and dusting you off again when you stumble along the way.

Equally, if there are people in your life who are consistently eating away at your self-confidence, it can have the opposite effect and tip the scales towards your no longer believing that you can achieve the goals you have set yourself.

You'd be surprised how negative people come out of the woodwork when you announce that you are actively seeking to make positive changes in your life – and will do all they can to hold you back.

Think about the people in your life. Do they support you 100% and provide constructive advice and feedback? Will they cheer you on to win? Will they celebrate your successes and encourage you when you encounter setbacks?

Who will you choose to have on your own personal Success Team?

Who do you know who could help YOU to achieve your goals? Why not start your own Success Team today with a handful of supportive friends or colleagues.

ೞ಄ఌ಄ఌ಄ఌ಄ఌ಄ఌ಄ఌ಄

"What is without
periods of rest
will not endure."

Ovid

ೞ಄ఌ಄ఌ಄ఌ಄ఌ಄ఌ಄ఌ಄

37. Take a Break!

You've been sitting for several minutes staring blankly at the same page of a book, the same computer screen, or a particular piece of work, but you don't seem to be able to concentrate or make any progress? Sound familiar?

When you find that your focus is dwindling this is your body giving you a big hint that it's time to take a break. Here are some tips for making any break you take more effective:

The best type of breaks entail not only changing the type of activity you're doing, but also your location. So, if you've been working at the computer in your office, it might be beneficial to stand up and stretch or, if feasible, take a walk round the block.

Avoid confusing 'diversions' with 'breaks'. For example, if you're working on the computer and you take a 'break' by playing computer games, you've only created a diversion, not a true break. Remember, an effective break requires a change of both location and activity.

Move your body! Exercise promotes the circulation, which increases the amount of oxygen in the brain – this helps to keep you alert and thinking clearly.

Get outside for some fresh air – and hopefully some sunshine. This is a great way to relax your mind and clear your thoughts.

Programme periodic breaks in your schedule throughout the day. Planning breaks in advance helps you to create a rhythm and balance to your schedule as well as keeping you refreshed.

(Taken from The Art of Taking a Break by Bernice Ross & Byron Van Arsdale)

"Your happiness depends on
three things, all of which are
within your power;
your will,
your ideas concerning
the events in which you
are involved,
and the use you make
of your ideas."

Epicetus

38. Capture Your Ideas

Ideas are precious.
They are to be kept, treasured and nurtured.

You know how it is. You have a fantastic idea, but you're rushing somewhere, or you're simply too busy and you don't get a chance to write it down and then it vanishes like a dream at the moment of waking.

As a writer, I have, for many years, adopted the habit of having a small notebook which I carry everywhere with me. You just never know when you'll overhear a snippet of a conversation or see a drama unfold before you which might come in handy for a story at some point in the future.

So here's your tip for this week. Buy yourself a book where you can store each and every idea you think of. It will need to be instantly accessible, yet small enough to carry around with you. Maybe you'll have two – one for the home or office and one for when you're out and about. I've been told – though I don't know if it's true – that Richard Branson has eight!

The thing about ideas is that even if they seem irrelevant or impossible at the time, they may very well leap into relevance months or even years later.

Capture your ideas. Don't let them float away. You never know when you might need them.

"Maintaining a complicated life is
a great way to avoid changing it."

Elaine St. James

39. What Are You Avoiding?

Is your life excessively busy? Do you feel as if you wake up in the morning and step straight onto the hamster wheel, be it at home or at work? Are you always rushing around and constantly trying to catch up? Is your life unnecessarily complicated?

Making ourselves BUSY can be the most wonderfully clever strategy for avoiding something that really needs attention in our lives. If this sounds as if it might be true for you, then ask yourself: "Is there something important that I'm effectively avoiding?"

Give yourself time to think about this – it may not be an easy admission to make.

This issue cropped up for me last year, and I have been consciously carving out time for myself to concentrate on the questions that surfaced as a result. These were not questions that could be easily answered – no wonder I had managed to avoid them so successfully for so long by making myself so 'busy'!!!

ೞೕ೯ೕ೯ೕ೯ೕ೯ೕ೯ೕ೯ೕ೯ೕ೯ೝ

"To live a creative life,
we must lose
our fear of being wrong."

Joseph Chilton Pearce

ೞೕ೯ೕ೯ೕ೯ೕ೯ೕ೯ೕ೯ೕ೯ೕ೯ೝ

40. "If I REALLY had my way..."

I allowed myself to take just one personal development book with me on holiday this year. One question from the book really leapt out at me and I find that I just can't budge it – I keep thinking about it. The question was: "If I REALLY had my way I would ..."

There's something wonderful about this question. It leads you into a land of infinite possibilities – of dreams – it takes you back to being in that childlike state where everything feels completely possible.

Too often it can feel as if life in the 21st century is swamping and constricting us. We're just all too busy to dream and certainly too busy to act on our dreams. So, as we enter the final quarter of the year, here's an exercise which will allow you to carry on the optimism of the summer and dream a little ...

STEP ONE: Take a pen and paper and write "If I REALLY had my way, I'd ..." at the top of the page. Then write as many responses to it as you can. Have fun with it. Please don't edit or censor anything. Just scribble anything and everything that comes to mind no matter how ridiculous, wild or unachievable it may feel.

STEP TWO: At this point, perverse creatures that we are, common sense tends to kick in and our natural inclination is to throw up all kinds of objections. 'I couldn't possibly do that.' ~ 'That's an insane idea.' ~ 'I'm far too old to even think of attempting that.' ~ So, to bypass this, for each item you've written ask yourself:

"OK, so how COULD this be possible?' or "What part of this might be possible?". Embrace the possibilities.

STEP THREE: Choose at least one item from the list (more if you like) and formulate five action steps you can take towards making it a reality.

CS⊷⊷⊷⊷⊷⊷⊷⊷⊷⊷⊷⊷⊷SO

"And the day came when the risk
it took to remain tight in a bud
was more painful than the risk
it took to blossom."

Anaïs Nin

CS⊷⊷⊷⊷⊷⊷⊷⊷⊷⊷⊷⊷⊷SO

41. Comfort – Stretch – Panic Goals

People often talk about 'comfort zones' and the importance of edging ourselves out of them every now and again. Pushing the limits of your personal comfort zone is really challenging, but the effects are hugely rewarding. It expands your horizons, boosts your confidence and helps you to feel that you can take on ever bigger and better things.

I heard a nice expression about this just the other day – that after taking on a challenge and stretching yourself you literally 'step into a bigger footprint'.

Rather than thinking simply of 'being in your comfort zone' or not, it may help to give yourself three levels of challenge with respect to your goals. Comfort – Stretch – and Panic.

A Comfort Goal speaks for itself. It's something you feel comfortable with, you've probably done it before and it doesn't pose a particular challenge.

A Stretch Goal is something you probably haven't done before, and it definitely feels a bit scary.

A Panic Goal – well again, that speaks for itself. It's downright terrifying to contemplate!

Remember that one person's definition of 'comfort' could well be another person's definition of 'panic' and vice versa – it's a very individual thing. I know people who thrive on public speaking, whereas for me the thought of being the keynote speaker at a conference would send me into a state of paralysis!

Have you been drifting along in your comfort zone for too long? If so, maybe it's time to shake things up a bit.

My challenge to you this week is to make a list of at least 20 Stretch and Panic goals. Then choose three – and start taking action towards at least one this week. If nothing else, it should get the adrenaline pumping.

ଔ᰾ᰕ᰾ᰕ᰾ᰕ᰾ᰕ᰾ᰕ᰾ᰕ᰾ᰕ᰾ᰕ᰾ᰕ᰾ᰔᰕ

"Success is knowing that if today
were your last day on earth you
could leave without regret."

Sarah Ban Breathnach

ଔ᰾ᰕ᰾ᰕ᰾ᰕ᰾ᰕ᰾ᰕ᰾ᰕ᰾ᰕ᰾ᰕ᰾ᰕ᰾ᰔᰕ

42. Completions

This week's Tip comes from a very personal experience. A few years ago I learned that my ex-mother-in-law had died. I was very fond of her, and had always felt sad that the break up of my marriage had resulted in my estrangement from her and my father-in-law.

Every now and again over the years I would think to myself that I really must make the effort to go to London and pop in and see them. I knew that they held no animosity towards me and it would have been really good to repair any misunderstandings that might have taken place, and restore what had once been a close relationship.

I never did it. Now, of course, it's too late and I regret that I never made the time.

- Is there anyone in your life that you would dearly like to have such a meeting – or such a conversation with?

- What do you need to say?

If there are any 'incomplete' situations in your life, why not make the effort to do whatever you have to do to feel 'complete' once more? It may not feel very comfortable, but you'll be very glad that you did.

"He who possesses most
must be most afraid of loss."

Leonardo Da Vinci

43. Decluttering

There's nothing like a really good clear out to make you feel great and to literally and metaphorically 'clear some space' in your life.

If your home or office needs a visit from the Decluttering Police, here are a few tips to help you to be ruthless about those items you are finding it hard to make a decision about.

Paper Mountain: It can be really hard to throw pieces of paper away – especially when the phrase "but I might need to refer to it later" keeps playing in your head. The most useful tip I've come across is to ask yourself – If I did need this in the future, is there some way that I could get hold of it again? In other words, could you ask the person who sent it to you to send you another copy? Could you download the information from the internet? Could you somehow reproduce the information in another way? If the answer is 'yes' it's a lot easier to make the decision to throw it away.

Clothing, books and other items: If you're finding it difficult to throw or give something away, try this trick. Get a bin liner, put the items into it, tie it up, put the date on the outside and store it somewhere like the garage or a shed. If you haven't needed any of the items within twelve months, throw the bag away (or give it to charity) – WITHOUT LOOKING INSIDE!

Ask for help: If you're still short on will power, choose a friend or colleague who you know to be decisive and ask them to help you. It's much easier for an outsider to be ruthless.

Hold a Decluttering Party: Make it fun! Get in some treats, and invite some friends round to help you decide which things to keep or which to get rid of. You never know, they might even want to take some of the items off your hands for you!

"People who have no time
don't think.

The more you think,
the more time you have."

Henry Ford

44. Busy vs. Productive

One of the most common complaints I hear from people is that they are just 'too busy'. There's too much to do and not enough hours in the day to do it in.

There's a very clear distinction between being 'busy' and being 'productive'. In some cases we make ourselves busy in order to avoid doing those things that may be more demanding, but really important — or to shield us from having to confront uncomfortable personal issues (see Tip 39).

Over the next week, notice when you are busy and ask yourself: Are the things you are doing truly productive? Could you actually delegate some of those tasks, or even drop them altogether? Are you caught up in Time Wasters? If so, be ruthless about dropping those activities and concentrate instead on things that are really going to produce a result.

Extra Tip!

How about coming up with an instant scoring system? Give yourself a mark out of ten on each of the things you find yourself doing throughout the day. If you can't give it more than a '5' then think seriously about not doing it and moving on to something more productive.

છ৹ళ৹ళ৹ళ৹ళ৹৵৹৵৹৵৹৵৹৵ৡ

"When I stand before God at
the end of my life, I would hope
that I would not have a single
talent left, and could say, 'I used
everything you gave me.'"

Erma Bombeck

છ৹ళ৹ళ৹ళ৹ళ৹৵৹৵৹৵৹৵৹৵ৡ

45. I Would Pick More Daisies

This week's Tip is taken from "The Procrastinator's Handbook" by Rita Emmett, and is written by Nadine Stair of Louisville, Kentucky. Nadine Stair was 85 years old when she wrote this:

"I'd dare to make more mistakes next time. I'd relax. I would limber up. I would be sillier than I have been this trip. I would take fewer things seriously. I would take more chances. I would take more trips. I would climb more mountains and swim more rivers. I would eat more ice cream and less beans. I would perhaps have more actual troubles, but I'd have fewer imaginary ones.

You see, I'm one of those people who live sensibly and sanely hour after hour, day after day. Oh, I've had my moments, and if I had it to do over again, I'd have more of them. In fact, I'd try to have nothing else. Just moments. One after another, instead of living so many years ahead of each day.

I've been one of those people who never go anywhere without a thermometer, a hot water bottle, a raincoat and a parachute. If I had it to do again, I would travel lighter next time.

If I had my life to live over, I would start barefoot earlier in the spring and stay that way later in the autumn. I would go to more dances. I would ride more merry-go-rounds. I would pick more daisies."

ᘓᔆᘏᔆᘏᔆᘏᔆᘏᔆᘏᔆᘏᔆᘏᔆᘏᔆᘐ

"Abundance is not
something we acquire.

It is something
we tune into."

Wayne Dyer

ᘓᔆᘏᔆᘏᔆᘏᔆᘏᔆᘏᔆᘏᔆᘏᔆᘏᔆᘐ

46. Creating Reserves

When I first started in business I had an inkjet printer which consumed ink cartridges at an alarming rate. Because they were so expensive, I tended to buy them one at a time, but in the back of my mind was a constant nagging worry that at any minute the ink would run out and I'd be left high and dry.

Eventually I decided that I was expending far too much energy worrying about this, so I bit the bullet and bought a stack of them to have in reserve. It's incredible the difference this made – no longer worrying if I was about to run out – no longer having 'just enough' but instead creating a safety cushion for myself.

The idea behind creating reserves is that you always have 'more than enough' rather than teetering on the brink of having 'only just enough'. Not wasting valuable energy worrying about not having enough can be immensely liberating – you will feel significantly calmer and more in control, and you will be working from a position of strength rather than a position of need.

Here are some other examples:

- Always have ample petrol in your tank
- Make sure you have sufficient money available for unexpected emergency expenditures
- Leave early for appointments so that you never have to rush or panic about being late
- Get lots of sleep so that you have reserves of energy
- Book social events into the diary on a regular basis to be sure that you have a sufficient reserve of FUN!

Where do YOU need to create reserves?

CR€€€€€€€€€€€€€€€€€

"One cannot give what he does
not possess. To give love you
must possess love. To love others
you must love yourself."

Leo Buscaglia

CR€€€€€€€€€€€€€€€€€

47. The Oxygen Mask Analogy

Do you – hand on heart – take enough time out for yourself? I'm becoming more and more convinced of how important it is to give yourself ample 'down time' in order to relax, switch your brain off from work and recharge your batteries.

I've noticed that many of the women that I work with – especially those with young families – find it a real challenge to take any time out for themselves. They've got into the habit of putting everyone else's needs first and can't see how they can carve out any 'me time'.

The self-employed can be equally challenged. I know only too well the perils of running your own business – how all consuming it can be – and how very hard it can be to switch your brain off from thinking about work.

Here's a great analogy: If you've flown on a commercial airliner you'll be familiar with the 'oxygen mask' demonstration and you'll probably have noticed that they always instruct you to make sure that your own mask is fitted before seeing to your children? Well, in life the same principle applies. You NEED to take care of yourself first in order to be able to care for those around you – be it your family, your friends or your clients. You just can't work as effectively if you're exhausted and drained.

So, for the next week, see if you can find a way to make some space for yourself – you may have to get a bit creative and enlist the help and support of others – family, friends – to allow you to have some 'down time' – even if it's just a Sunday morning or an evening to yourself.

Put on your oxygen mask, breathe deeply, and have a great week!

"The path to financial freedom
can be long and challenging.
The commitment to become
responsible with money is the
key that opens the flood gates
to more."

Cheryl Richardson

48. Festive Finance

Incredible though it may seem, Christmas really is just around the corner. Inevitably, it's a very expensive time of year, and in the heat of the moment it's easy to spend more than we can really afford.

Here's a tip to help ensure there are some extra funds available for the Festive Season, but it can also be applied throughout the rest of the year.

Do you know how much you spend in a week or a month? Do you know what you spend your money on? One way to keep tabs on this is to keep a Spending Log for a week or two – just to see where your hard-earned money is actually going. You might be in for a few surprises.

A friend of mine tried this out and was shocked to discover that she was spending, on average, £30 a week on Cappuccinos – that's a whopping £120 per month.

Another was equally shocked to realise he had a wine bill approaching £200 per month.

By becoming aware of how you're spending your money, you can take control of it. You can then decide whether to forego a Latte or two in order to have the extra funds you need to afford something special (not to mention improve your health and well-being) – or, more importantly, to avoid going into the red over the Holiday Season.

"Take your life in your own
hands and what happens?

A terrible thing:
no one to blame."

Erica Jong

49. Watch your Language

What kind of image do you portray to the outside world? Many factors combine to define how we appear to others: how we dress, our body language, our posture, our attitude.

Another factor which determines how others perceive us is the way we speak. Not only the tenor or strength of our voice, but the language we use.

Some people really let themselves down by using unassertive and self-deprecating language. Phrases like: "Oh trust me to get that wrong" or "I'm really hopeless at ...." or "Don't ask me to do 'x' – I'm bound to mess it up..." give a very clear message about your view of yourself and your abilities.

Self-deprecation is a very 'British' thing to do – to make light of your abilities and achievements. But while it's great to be able to laugh at yourself and not take things too seriously, it should never be at the expense of your self-confidence.

If we want people to take us seriously, and to see us as a competent person, it's really important to exude a confident persona (even if we don't always feel it!) and part of that is NOT putting ourselves down in front of others. In fact, don't put yourself down ever – most especially to yourself.

So here's an experiment: For the next week just NOTICE each time you use – or are about to use – self-deprecating language. Count the number of times you do it. Then make a conscious choice to stop. If it's an old, ingrained habit, it may take a while to break, but it's really worth it.

You are fantastic, capable, wise, creative, clever, powerful and strong. Don't let your language say otherwise.

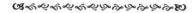

"In our African language we say
'a person is a person through
other persons.' ...

We are made for a delicate
network of relationship, of
interdependence. We are meant
to complement each other. All
kinds of things go horribly wrong
when we break that fundamental
law of our being."

Desmond Tutu

50. Emotional Bank Account

Those of you who have read Stephen Covey's book "The Seven Habits of Highly Effective People" will recognise this term. Covey suggests that in our relationships we build up a strong and healthy 'bank account' with others by consistently 'making deposits' through acts of kindness, consideration, honesty, keeping commitments, thoughtfulness and so on. Equally, by treating someone unkindly, criticising, breaking promises, betraying trust, your account diminishes and is in danger of becoming overdrawn.

One of the ways Covey suggests to build up your bank account with the special people in your life is through Understanding the Individual. Part of this is understanding that what might constitute a deposit for you, might not do so for them. It also means making what is important to the other person as important to you.

Covey writes: "I have a friend whose son developed an avid interest in baseball. My friend wasn't interested in baseball at all. But one summer, he took his son to see every major league team play one game. The trip took over six weeks and cost a great deal of money.
My friend was asked on his return, 'Do you like baseball that much?'
'No', he replied, 'But I like my son that much'... "

This had a profound impact on me when I read it. For years my partner and I have been engaged in a bit of a power struggle over cleaning the house! A spotless house is very important to him, and I had tended to rebel when he wanted me to make more of an effort in that direction. Reading Covey's words stopped me in my tracks. His desire for a clean house suddenly became more important to me as well.

Is there some way that you can apply this to your life this week?

CRQ❧❧❧❧❧❧❧❧❧❧❧❧❧❧BR

"As a silversmith sifts dust
from silver, remove your own
imbalances little by little."

The Dhammapada

CRQ❧❧❧❧❧❧❧❧❧❧❧❧❧❧BR

51. Patterns

"Awareness is the precursor of change"

When we stop and think about it, we can probably recognize many different behaviour patterns in our lives. Some of these might be having a positive influence, whilst others could be doing quite the opposite. With the holiday season fast approaching, it can be valuable to take a few minutes to think about some of your behaviour patterns. Congratulate yourself on those that are likely to contribute positively to your enjoyment of the festivities – and take an honest look at those patterns which are likely to produce less positive results.

- Do you tend to run yourself ragged as a result of other people's expectations?
- Do you tend to eat or drink far too much over Christmas and the New Year and neglect doing any exercise?
- Do you take the love and support of those round you for granted?
- Do you over-spend and then have to spend months repairing the damage to your bank account or overdraft?

Step One: Make yourself AWARE of existing patterns.

Step Two: Recognize that you have a CHOICE:

a) to continue the existing pattern, or

b) to consciously let it go and adopt a new pattern that serves you better.

What new and improved patterns – ones that will serve you well – do you want to take with you into the New Year?

"Look not mournfully into the Past.
It comes not back again.

Wisely improve the Present.
It is thine.

Go forth to meet the shadowy Future,
without fear and with a manly heart."

Elaine St. James

52. Your One-Year Vision

As one year finishes and another is about to begin, this can be an ideal time to do some thinking about what you would like to achieve in the year to come.

One of the most effective ways to do this is to take yourself out of the present and transport yourself into the future. Rather than think about what you would like to happen in the coming year, transport yourself to the end of next year and imagine that everything you wanted to achieve has already happened. What will your life look like in a year's time? What are you doing? Where are you? Who are you with? What have you achieved? Make this as detailed and vivid as you can. And THINK BIG! Don't limit yourself. The key is to write your vision in the PRESENT TENSE – as if it has already happened.

You can use narrative, lists, bullet points or pictures to describe what your life will look like. Or cut out pictures, phrases and captions from magazines. Have fun, get creative and again – think big.

It's quite miraculous how powerful this exercise can be. Over and over again I've been thrilled to witness a client's delight and amazement when they revisit their one-year vision and realise that they've achieved everything they had envisioned – and much more!

So if you want the next year to be a raving success, my Tip for this week is to get started on your One Year Vision. Have fun with it – you could even get the family involved, and do a 'Family Vision' together. If you want to take this further, once your vision is finished, you can divide the year into smaller segments. In other words, to achieve your one-year vision, what would you need to have done in 6 months? 3 months? The next month? Keep working on it and seek support if you need it.

Wishing you a happy and peaceful Festive Season and all good things in the year to come!

References

Books

Feel the Fear and Do It Anyway, Susan Jeffers,
   published 1987, by Random House Books.

First Things First, Stephen R Covey,
   published 1994 by Simon and Schuster.

Leadership from the Inside Out, Kevin Cashman,
   published 2000 by Executive Excellence Publishing.

Your Best Year Yet, Jinny S Ditzer,
   published 1994 by Thorsons.

Pure Bliss: The Art of Living in Soft Time, Gill Edwards,
   published 2006 by Piatkus.

The Procrastinator's Handbook, Rita Emmett,
   published 2001 by Fusion Press (Satin Publications Ltd).

7 Habits of Highly Effective People, Stephen R Covey,
   published 1989 by Simon and Schuster.

Coaches Mentioned

Mark Forster – The Time Freedom Coach
   Tel: +44 (0)1403-250016 www.markforster.net

Mark's books
   Get Everything Done and Still Have Time to Play (2000)
   and How To Make Your Dreams Come True (2002) are
   published by Hodder & Stoughton.

'Verbal Paper Cuts' and 'Take A Break!' are based on original
   articles by Bernice Ross and Byron Van Arsdale
   www.Teleclass4U.com

What Readers Say...

Inspired and yet so simple. Annabel's coaching tips are always a joy – written with a lightness of touch and a personal style that makes me feel she's writing them just for me!

Sue Robinson

These tips really provide practical and easy to follow steps to handle the stuff that often gets in the way of how we want things to be. They are easy to apply which means that they really work and make an immediate difference. Simply wonderful.

Ali Giblin, Career & Business Coach

Annabel's coaching tips are original and practical. They give me a focus and have helped me to overcome the every day challenges that life throws up.

Blaire Palmer, Managing Director

The wonderful thing about your tips: We knew these pearls all along. But without your reminding us, they would have stayed way down there on the ocean floor. Thanks!

Helyn Connor

Annabel's coaching tips bring a breath of fresh air on many a hot day. If I need something to remind me to focus on the key issues in my life I have found that they often hit the nail on the head.

Stephen G Baker, Private Banker with HBOS

Annabel's inspiring tips have enabled me to realise that there really is an exciting life out there – a journey full of opportunities and experiences and that it really is OK to 'go for it!'.

Sarah Dawson, Reflexologist

Your tips are like having a best friend – they bring your life back into focus, they encourage you to tackle challenging issues quickly and they boost your confidence. In short, they help you make the most of life.

Jane Bleakley